JUL 2012

OKLAHOMA

A SENSE OF PLACE

MICHAEL WALLIS

digitature

ISBN-13: 978-0615626598
ISBN-10: 0615626599

Cover Art by Jeremy Luther
Cover & Book Design by Connor Raus
Author Photo by Emily Priddy

Digitature
118 Waverly Place
New York, New York 10011
http://www.digitature.com

For all angels in disguise and
foot-loose ghosts

ABOUT

On January 6, 2012, best-selling author Michael
Wallis was the featured speaker at the Tulsa Town
Hall Speaker Series, 77th Season. Wallis spoke to a
capacity crowd at the 2300 seat Chapman Music
Hall of the Performing Arts Center in downtown
Tulsa, Oklahoma. The original title of the address
— "Way Down Yonder in the Indian Nation" — has
been changed to "Oklahoma: A Sense of Place," to
distinguish it from the title of another Wallis book.
At the conclusion of the speech, the audience rose as
one with a thunderous and sustained standing
ovation. In the weeks following his appearance,
Wallis received numerous tributes, letters and

messages of praise, and accolades from throughout Oklahoma and beyond. He also was besieged by requests for a copy of his remarks. That led to the creation of this book.

INTRODUCTION

Introduction of Michael Wallis, January 6, 2012, at Tulsa Town Hall in the Chapman Music Hall of the Tulsa Performing Arts Center.

Good morning, I am Mary Ann Lewis on behalf of the Tulsa Town Hall board. Welcome all of you to this third lecture in our 77th season.

It is a special pleasure to introduce our speaker Michael Wallis, who has been a Tulsa resident since 1982. Curiosity begs the question, why or how does someone become an author? The answer for Michael Wallis begins with a special experience at the age of eleven when he won an essay contest sponsored by

AAA, on the topic of what it meant to be a school patrol boy. His prize was a limousine ride and tickets to a St. Louis Cardinals game at Sportsman's Park. He was thrilled to be given a special seat in the Cardinal dugout, placed between third baseman Kenny Boyer and outfielder Stan "The Man" Musial. On his ride home, clutching a signed baseball from his Cardinal heroes, the young Wallis realized that "this writing was not a bad deal."

As a young adult our author lived in a Hemingway fashion. After a stint in the U.S. Marines he resided in Santa Fe, New Mexico, and became immersed in an artist colony of the time while working in various jobs such as a ranch hand, hotel waiter, bartender, and ski lodge manager.

In 1976 he became special correspondent for Time-Life and spent two years in the Florida Caribbean Bureau, covering the Cuban refugee exodus as well as drug smuggling and crime. It was in 1988 that he wrote his first book *Oil Man* that led to a gusher of 16 additional books and three Pulitzer Prize nominations.

Michael Wallis is a born storyteller who views all of life experiences as adventures. For him, people are books. He loves bringing out unique stories from truck drivers, pie-serving waitresses, barbecue joint pit masters, oilmen, and cowboys. As a passionate historian he writes with such descriptive richness that the reader's senses are fully engaged in getting to know the men and women of the American West. The scent of wood smoke, the images of moonless nights and the taste of bear meat and venison are so vivid that one is quickly transported from modern life into the wild and wonderful world of his biographies.

Michael's fascination with Route 66 led to its revitalization, and his book *Route 66: The Mother Road* is recognized for establishing the Chicago to Los Angeles highway's historical prominence. He led the Pixar Studio's artistic team on research tours of the highway before the making of the beloved movie *Cars*. His deep husky voice has defined the personality of the Sheriff in both *Cars* and its sequel. Michael and his wife Suzanne Fitzgerald Wallis co-authored the book *The Art of Cars*. Suzanne is always acknowledged in all of Michael's literary works as his magician who is an integral part of the creative process. The enchantment in our speaker's writing is his portrayal of a variety of personalities and historic

figures and how vibrantly he makes them live again.
Can't you just imagine David Crocket standing here,
stage left, with his long rifle; or Billy the kid perched
on the mezzanine railing; or "Pretty Boy" Floyd
slouching by the exit door ready to escape if the need
should arise? I like to think that all of his characters
are quietly present amidst this Performing Arts
Center audience, eagerly awaiting the writer's
presentation.

Please join me in welcoming Mr. Michael Wallis,
one of our nation's premier historians.

OKLAHOMA: A SENSE OF PLACE

Once upon a time, there was no state of Oklahoma, no Indian Territory — and nobody knew the difference. There was always, however, this land, this place.

Long before the arrival of the first tribal people, the nomadic warriors and hunters, the adventurers, the conquered tribes with their slaves, the outlaws and misfits, the land-hungry sodbusters, the oil barons, and all the rest, this land was a clean canvas.

There were no towns or cities, no roads or highways, no jailhouses, cemeteries, casinos, marinas, or country clubs. The grassland meadows and old-growth timber were the temples and cathedrals. The mountains, hills, valleys, and hidden hollows near clear creeks were the universities and schools. The best entertainment came from prairie light shows — spectacular concerts of thunder, lightning, and wind.

Then change came. The land evolved from being a place where a vast variety of land-life forms met and mingled — a true transition zone — to become a crossroads for human traffic.

Thankfully, there are still remnants from the past. There are still isolated places that survive as a tribute to long ago, when the odds were in favor of the wild creatures. These places survive to teach and remind. They survive to help us understand what we have lost and what could still be lost unless we dare to imagine and to remember. Unless we truly appreciate our sense of place.

A sense of place is more than geography. And certainly not every place has a sense of place. Those places that are lacking can be called "placeless" or "inauthentic." They are landscapes with no special relationship to their locale — they could be anywhere. Good examples are shopping malls, strip centers, fast food chains and other manifestations of generic America. Even some historic sites have been diluted and heavily commercialized for tourism and in so doing have lost their sense of place.

Sense of place is important because it offers you a sense of belonging and being which are essential parts of life. For many, perhaps some of you, a sense of place is a feeling you get when you belong somewhere. It is a place that you cherish no matter where it may be.

Most people would say this sense of place belongs to their hometown, where they grew up, or, experienced the best years of their life. For others, it may be a place they have only visited or lived a short time, yet this place gives them a feeling of belonging, which their home cannot provide.

During the nineteenth century, Oklahoma occupied a strategic but peculiar place in the national life. As a special federal territory, it served the national purpose as a military-defense frontier. Most of the early non-Indians who came here were soldiers manning the various forts and military posts. No soldiers remained long enough to develop a "sense of place."

By 1890, Indian Territory had become the home of 67 different tribes from all sections of the continental United States. Then once they were relocated here, mostly under duress, many of the tribes were moved again to make room for others, thus discouraging any sense of attachment to land so far from their native homes.

As always there were exceptions. When the Creeks started on their forced journey from their Alabama home to Indian Territory, they carried an earthen pot filled with ashes and embers from their council fire and a firebrand. Each night when they pitched camp, the Creeks ignited a new council fire with the brand and the following morning a new brand was taken to light a fire again that night. The fires were rekindled in this way all along the route from the banks of the Chattahoochee to the bluffs of the Arkansas River.

The Creeks made their way through vines and brush and trudged up a low rise overlooking the east bank of the broad Arkansas. Beneath the boughs of a stout post oak tree, they deposited the ashes they had carried from Alabama. Then as darkness fell, they kindled a new council fire. They paid tribute to the land they left behind and the many family members who perished during the two-year journey. "This is our new home," principal chief Achee Yahola was said to have told his people. At that instant, with long shadows dancing in the glow of fresh flames sparked from the ashes and coals, Tulsa was created. The Creeks had brought a sense of place with them and their leader was right — now this land truly was their new home.

"It was a strange beginning for a modern city," Angie Debo wrote many years after that brief shining moment. "The flickering fire, the silent valley, the dark intent faces, and the wild cadence of ritual."

Despite the seemingly smooth transition of the Creeks, their struggles and those of other tribal people were far from over. Only ten years after the Creeks arrival, the jingoistic term "Manifest Destiny" had become a rallying cry with politicians who believed the United States had a divine mandate to expand from "sea to shining sea." This concept galvanized proponents of expansion and pro-slavery Southerners eager to increase their domain. The resulting years of turmoil and war shook this land. It became uneven, out of step, and without any rhythm. Without rhythm there can be no balance. Still, despite the human and natural toll, this land was tempered by the violence and discord.

A well-balanced and wise Wallace Stegner said it best: "No place is a place until things that have happened in it are remembered in history, ballads, yarns, legends, or monuments... History was part of the baggage we threw overboard when we launched ourselves into the New World. We threw it away because it recalled old tyrannies, old limitations, galling obligations, bloody memories. Plunging into the future through a landscape that had no history, we did both the country and ourselves some harm along with the good. Neither the country nor the society we built out of it can be healthy until we stop raiding and running, and learn to be quiet part of the time, and acquire the sense not of ownership but of belonging."

How does the song go? "We know we belong to the land, and the land we belong to is grand!" But do we really know that? Sometimes I wonder.

As a writer of American history and culture and a human geographer, nothing matters more to me than "a sense of place" and the opportunity to wander through the places where my subjects lived. Although usually the landscape has changed and the people themselves are long gone, I envision them in their own surroundings and know their essence remains forever and ever.

I stalk the dimensions of the old 101 Ranch where grizzled cowboys rode with Tom Mix and Bill Pickett, and looked into the eyes of Buffalo Bill and Geronimo. I find a 90-year old retired one-legged bank robber in his air stream trailer tucked away in a bootlegger's hollow where many men and any number of soiled doves met violent deaths.

I catch a whiff of the blended aroma of Frank Phillips' bay rum and cigars, the scent of Pretty Boy's pomade, the smell of a thousand Route 66 blue-plate specials, or the perfume of ancient peonies in a garden once tended by Thomas Gilcrease.

I watch a spindly walking stick make its way up Wilma Mankiller's shoulder and start up her hair, as Wilma gently shakes the creature free. I see Will Rogers grinning on the stage at Miami's Coleman Theater, Quanah Parker's stoic gaze, and a young Tony Randall racing from the Sophian Plaza, late again for class at old Central High School.

I memorize the music of Woody Guthrie, a national treasure — just a boy from Oklahoma on an endless one-night stand.

I listen to the voices of the unnamed and unsung.

I hear the crowd roar when eight eternal seconds pass while Freckles Brown rides the back of Tornado, the toughest rodeo bull that ever came out of a chute.

I hear the poetry and song coming from the varicose and scarred lanes of the Mother Road. And I smile when the grand tune "Oklahoma Hills" tumbles out the door at Cain's Ballroom.

"Many months have come and gone
since I wandered from my home,
In those Oklahoma Hills where I was born.
Tho' a page of life has turned,

And a lesson I have learned,

Yet I feel in those hills I still belong.

Way down yonder in the Indian Nation,

I rode my pony on the reservation,

In those Oklahoma Hills where I was born.

Way down yonder in the Indian Nation,

A cowboy's life is my occupation,

In those Oklahoma Hills where I was born."

I was not born in those Oklahoma Hills but it is here that I belong. For it is here I have a sense of place. I came to this place many years past as a fully-grown man with my wife Suzanne. We made the conscious decision to adopt this land and make it our home. I was born and raised in Missouri. I have always looked westward, I bleed St. Louis Cardinal red, I prefer two-lane roads to turnpikes, I consider rhubarb pie sacred, and I believe in ghosts and trust in angels.

That was true when I was a boy watching my mother find work for the dusty men of the open road who came off the old alignment of Route 66 near our place. They'd appear at the back door and doff their caps; looking to do some work in exchange for some food. My mother always found work for them. And then she fed them and as they ate in the shade of the yard I stood on a chair by my mother's side at the sink and we watched from the window. The men ate, and we made up stories about them. We gave them names and decided where they had come from and where they were going. That was how I first learned about story telling.

When the men finished eating, they gave my mother the dishes and thanked her and then walked off — out of our lives back to the Mother Road. And every time, every time, my Mother would tell me: "Son, you must remember this — never ever turn anyone away from your door. They may be angels — angels in disguise." Her words stay with me to this day.

In this land — right here — Way Down Yonder in the Indian Nation — I have found many angels in disguise and plenty of ghosts as well.

Footloose ghosts are everywhere. They are at large all across the land, stalking the prairies and valleys. They find cover among thickets of sumac, bois d'arc, sassafras, and persimmon, and they mingle in stands of cedar, walnut, honey locust, and sycamore. Ghosts roost along the banks of the contrary Arkansas, the sluggish Verdigris, the scenic Illinois, and a slew of tributary streams and creeks. Some ghosts perch on sharp bluffs or on lakeshores of Tenkiller, Oologah, Spavinaw, Eufaula, Skiatook, and Keystone. No ghosts at Grand Lake, too many people and powerboats.

Others scout the everlasting Osage Hills, studded with stubborn blackjack oaks. Phantoms peek from the shadows of deserted oil rigs and derelict buildings. Restless spirits rattle in the winter wind.

Specters from long ago and others from only yesterday patrol the boulevards and alleys of Tulsa, Muskogee, Tahlequah, Bartlesville, and Commerce, and frequent the parks, museums, and churches of those cities. They sleep right here in the orchestra pit, at the top of towering catalpa trees, in clumps of fiery azaleas and, like purring cats, on windowsills of homes built before there was an Oklahoma. They congregate in small-town cafes, courthouse squares, and schoolyards at Okmulgee, Sapulpa, Poteau,

Sallisaw, Heavener, Checotah, Pawnee, and scores of burgs no bigger than a minute.

Timeless sentinels — serene as a Sunday morning benediction — visit empty oil patch towns, farms and ranches, pecan groves, melon patches, and stockyards. They straddle rodeo fences, hang out at beer joints, kibitz over backgammon boards, eavesdrop at every cafe's liar's table, hover in the upper reaches of corporate palaces, and, like most self-respecting ghosts, gather with pals in country graveyards.

Mostly they go unnoticed and unheard, mistaken for shifting evening shade, a coyote's distant song, the twilight serenade of a mockingbird, summer breeze caressing an ocean of big bluestem. They are confused for shooting stars streaking the night

heavens or for renegade tornadoes spawned by
humid air floating up from the Gulf of Mexico,
colliding on the prairies with the old winds of spring
sweeping down from the north.

It is only fitting that the distinct countryside and
communities of old Indian Territory provide
sanctuary to so many ghosts. This great expanse of
land always has been part of the restlessness that
pushed people across North America in persistent
quest of richer soils, the earth's treasure, better
opportunities, and a new beginning.

If the broad western plains and golden wheat fields
— where winds are born — act as the lusty lungs of
the state, then the vibrant heart of Oklahoma lies
here in old Indian Territory, where so many traces,

trails, paths, and highways converge and become the crossroads of the nation.

You could say I truly discovered this crossroads in the sweltering summer of 1980 while I was working out of the Caribbean Bureau in Miami for Time-Life and I had occasion to spend some time in Tulsa. I was hunting a good story and was nested at the Mayo Hotel with plenty of ice and the AC set so low I could see my breath.

One late afternoon, I moseyed down to the Arkansas River to have a look. Long before there was a Tulsa, there was the river — the longest tributary in the Mississippi-Missouri system. Near its headwaters in the Colorado Rockies at Tennessee Pass on the eastern slope of the continental divide, glacial lakes and snowmelt feed the river before it flows 1,450 miles southeast through Colorado, Kansas, Oklahoma, and Arkansas.

Given to rampaging tantrums, the river was historically as moody as a water moccasin and just as cruel. A temperamental river prone to devastating floods, the Arkansas dared to be tamed. That, of course, finally happened but for many years the river did as it pleased and Tulsans gave the muddy waters their respect. For the Arkansas is rich in history. Indians bathed their ponies in the river, adventurers camped on the sandbars, and cowboys paraded cattle through the shallows.

Zebulon Pike explored the Arkansas and in 1832 noted author Washington Irving chronicled the river's sand shore bordered by cottonwoods and willows as he made his famous tour of the prairies.

Irving and his entourage rode the banks of the Arkansas and saw beaches and muddy banks marked by the hooves of Osage and Pawnee hunting parties.

They paused to quench their thirsts at the foot of the steep lawn of what we now know as the McBirney Mansion, built 95 years after Irving's journey by an Irish immigrant who struck it rich in black gold. Today cool water still pulses from the underground spring that surfaces there. Irving saw the sun shining through leaves tinted by autumn and was reminded of the stained glass and clustering columns of gothic cathedrals.

"The river scenery at this place was beautifully diversified, presenting long, shining reaches," Irving wrote in his journal. "It was a bright sunny morning, with a transparent atmosphere that seemed to bathe the very heart with gladness"

Generally known for his humorous rendition of romanticized tales, such as *Rip Van Winkle* and *The Legend of Sleepy Hollow*, Irving's prose turns out to be much more than sentimental travel writing, but rather a depiction of landscape that transcends the romantic frontier metaphor and sheds light on the environment's impact on Irving himself. While others viewed this land and its creatures as endless and something to be conquered and used, Irving became woefully aware of its infinite nature, something that some people today, particularly our Oklahoma politicians, still fail to comprehend. But on that hot June afternoon in 1980 when I made my own trek to hopefully catch a morsel of what Irving witnessed, I was more concerned with reaching the cool shade provided by the cottonwoods along the riverbank.

And it was there that I encountered a fellow who put me in mind of those silent men with empty eyes who occasionally appeared at the back door of my boyhood home in Missouri. Those "angels in disguise."

This fellow sitting beneath a gnarled cottonwood on the edge of the river had those same empty eyes. We nodded at each other and as we watched the sun lowering in the sky he spoke to me.

He told me he was pleased it was twilight and he was a day closer to dying. A long time ago, he had heard that a person could wear out his heart by sleeping on his left side. He said he had slept in that position ever since. He told me straight out that it had been years since he liked himself — almost a lifetime ago, when he was young and strong, and gave a damn.

He told me of his Cherokee lineage and of his growing up years in the Cherokee Nation. He said that he had been an Oklahoma cowboy and could ride, rope, and holler like a banshee. He made the circuits, mostly performing at the big Mother Road venues — Oklahoma City, Amarillo, Albuquerque, Flagstaff, Barstow, and many others. Then his life came all apart.

A crippling fall from a bucking bronco at a two-bit rodeo had left him with a broken back, a permanent limp, and a bad attitude. For good measure, a steady diet of ninety-proof whiskey stopped him from ever climbing into a saddle again.

The man allowed that he had lost everything. He had no more family, no more friends, and no more high-speed gallops on spirited cow ponies. He had no self-respect. It had been years since he looked in a mirror. He said he had become a street person — just a nice way of saying, "bum."

I walked a ways with the man. We headed up the trail toward the old alignment of Route 66 making its way across the chocolate colored river. We passed the spring at the McBirney Mansion and reached the old bridge. I recalled the many times I had sped across those waters on my way west chasing the sun and the moon and my dreams. We went below the bridge and the man showed me his makeshift camp of cardboard boxes and Goodwill blankets. Like the man, the bridge had been abandoned, but at one time it was the best way to go. It no longer was used for vehicular traffic, but sat neglected and forlorn next to a newer bridge.

Back on the trail again, we stopped and watched the river flowing past. Neither of us spoke for a long time. I let my thoughts take me back to the years before any bridges spanned the Arkansas. I considered the Creek people who came this way to build a new home and start their lives over. I thought about cattlemen herding hundreds of Texas longhorns across the rocky ford in the shallows of the river. I imagined the ferryboats loaded with passengers, and the first railroad bridge, erected back in the late 1800s. Then I recalled reading about the crude toll bridge that had been built in 1903. Workers and machines crossed it to get to the rich oil fields waiting on the other side, helping to assure Tulsa's future.

And then my mind brought me to Cy Avery —
Father of Route 66 — and the man who made sure
that the new highway came right through Tulsa and
how he used the 11th Street Bridge to make his case.

The street man and I walked on and went back to
the same place we had first met. We turned around
and looked up into the neighborhoods. Beyond I
spied the art deco towers dotting the skyline. The old
rodeo rider clutched a paper sack holding his few
worldly possessions — a broken pocket comb, some
raggedy underwear and socks, a sack of tobacco and
rolling papers, and a tarnished belt buckle the size of
a saucer which he had won long before at a rodeo.
There was also a good-sized tomato wrapped in
newspaper in the sack. He admitted to me that it had
been liberated from a backyard garden the night
before.

As we walked and swapped more stories, mostly about traveling the road, a morsel of survivor cried out from the man. He ignored the pleas of some passing pals to share their jug of vintage rotgut. Instead he picked up his pace and he told me he would go to a local mission for a hot supper and a shower and a night resting under cool sheets. He said all he had to do was endure a few hymns and listen to a fire-and-brimstone sermon delivered by a reformed drunk.

It was time for me to head back to the Mayo. We stopped in the shade and the man from the river — the bridge man — shook my hand and bade me farewell. But as he walked away, he stopped and turned. He reached in his sack and gave me his prized tomato and told me to enjoy it. He thanked me for spending time with him and helping him remember. Finally he said maybe he would sleep on his back for a while and give his tired heart a rest.

When he left, I bit into the tomato. It was vine ripened and warm and juicy and tasted of summer. The juice ran down my chin and droplets splattered on the red-hot sidewalk. When I looked up, the man was gone — making his way in a city that didn't know he existed.

Two years later I married Suzanne and we moved to Tulsa. That trip to Oklahoma to find a story had made an impression on me. I had fallen deeply in love with the state and the people. I felt I had a true sense of the place.

Not long after we moved here, I went down to the river and looked for the old cowboy. I roamed the shoreline and went down under the old 66 bridge. His camp was gone and there were a few young guys pan-cooking some fish. They didn't know any old cowboys.

The memory of that bridge man I met long ago stays with me. I find it slightly ironic that in this mineral-rich land that had produced so many oil millionaires, one of my dominant early recollections is of a salt-of-the-earth soul who was in my life for such a fleeting time and whose name I never knew. A Cherokee cowboy — who for a little while — lived beneath the Mother Road.

Never could find him. Not a trace. I still look sometimes when I head for home or cruise down 66. Maybe he was an angel in disguise.

But although the old rodeo rider is gone that bridge is still there. Despite the odds it has survived. There is a reason for that I am dead sure. That old span of concrete is a symbol of many layers of the Mother Road; it stands for the endurance and ingenuity of this country and of this state.

That place on the Arkansas is where the East collides with the West. That is where they meet. Right there. Right there where the bridge marks the spot.

Oklahoma is a relatively new and precocious state and so is Tulsa — a city that has always had more than its share of excitement and danger. That was true when we were a Creek settlement, a cow town, and the oil capitol of the world. For this place is tailor-made for risk takers. It is a land for people not allergic to hard work who are more than willing to take a chance. It has always been the risk takers who have broken through and changed things. They were willing to risk their reputations, relationships, and resources to get the job done.

Sometimes, to get the job done, rules were bent. Not all of your ancestors who slipped across the border were dressed like preachers and wearing sunbonnets. Speaking of headwear, in truth there were no white hats or black hats, but lots of gray hats. Never forget that four of the infamous Dalton brothers had been deputy marshals fed up with getting low wages for risking their lives. Before he started prospecting for oil, the Iowa barber turned risk taker Frank Phillips' first loan customer at his new bank in Bartlesville, was Henry Starr — self-proclaimed King of the Oklahoma bank robbers — who promptly paid back every last cent.

In the years after the Civil War, plenty of thieves, rapists, killers, and robbers found refuge in Indian Territory — many of them, I should point out, from my home state of Missouri. Indian Territory was a criminal's paradise and a legal and jurisdictional nightmare. One newspaper said this place was "the rendezvous of the vile and wicked from everywhere." Law-abiding residents were not immune to the outrages. Since many of the peace officers had once been outlaws or else ended up as felons, it seemed a very thin line separated good and evil. Indian Territory became known as the consummate robber's roost, and its sinister reputation spread across the country.

Eventually, wave after wave of white intruders and all stripes of anxious settlers eager to grab up a piece of land, raced into "the Nations." They built homes, established towns and businesses in what had been the domain of proud Indian people, who we had the audacity to label as the "Five Civilized Tribes," a pejorative and detestable name still in common use. What we often forget about is that according to the United States government this land was to remain forever "Indian Territory," free of white men altogether and for all time. That, of course, was never meant to be and starting in 1889, the various "runs," as they were known, ignited wholesale white settlement.

Besides the tribes, there were others who saw the land runs as questionable developments. On January 6, 1889 — 123 years ago today — a story was published in the New York Times under the simple headline, "The Truth About Oklahoma." It directly addressed the upcoming land run of 1889 and its implications.

"The accepted definition of the word settler in the West is one who enters a country to take up a farm," stated the Times. "Are there any such persons in the piratical mob that has gathered at Southern Kansas towns? I do not believe there is one. The men who have congregated at these towns are town-lot and village-site speculators. They are briefless and desperate lawyers, disappointed pothouse politicians, ruffians who have been blown from the dead towns of the arid zone by the fiery heat of Mexican winds... Settlers? Yes, in the vigorous vernacular of the plains they are settlers. They settle their enemies to rest. They settle town disputes with revolvers and repeating rifles... I have seen the men who make up these mobs. They are dirty and vicious and idle and ignorant and worthless. They are migratory ruffians who travel, and ever travel to escape from debts and labor. As a class they are tall, rawboned, mean of face, shuffling of gait. They are sand hillers and crackers of the arid plains and sneaking assassins who have shaken with swamp fever while lying out nights to kill their enemies from an ambush. Settlers! God save the country they settle in!"

Even back then many of the negative images which some people accept as accurate characterizations of Oklahoma were based on wholesale generalizations, misconceptions, and blatant twisting of the truth. Yet all too often we can be our worst enemies. Sometimes we are the ones most guilty of distorting the true image of Oklahoma. This can happen by rewriting or reinventing our own invaluable history or, even worse, by ignoring the past and conveniently disregarding all critical events, catastrophes, and controversies.

This denial of both the good and the bad episodes of history has always been a problem. It includes not only the sometimes murderous treatment of Indian people, but also the shameful Tulsa massacre of 1921, and other acts of sheer bigotry and blatant racial discrimination. Too often such events have been purged or swept under the carpet because of the perception that they reflected poorly on the land and the people.

Still, one of the most notable examples of modifying history is the reaction of many Oklahomans to the Great Depression and the dust-bowl years of the 1930s. In that bittersweet decade, the nation's economy cracked, and wholesale drought and destruction visited the land. Indelible scars were left on the earth and the people. A great migration of so-called Okies, Arkies, disenfranchised workers, broken dirt farmers, and vagabonds headed west to rebuild shattered dreams and start new lives in the promised land of California. Many of these refugees and migrants took to the Mother Road, as author John Steinbeck called Route 66 in his immortal novel, *The Grapes of Wrath*.

Viking published the book on April 14, 1939. Almost immediately after it first appeared, it became a lightning rod for controversy, criticism and conflict.

This novel, this work of pure genius penned by Steinbeck, tells in straightforward language and style the impassioned story of the fictional Joad family and their brutal migration from rural Oklahoma to

California's corrupt growing fields. The novel is a controversial classic — in some circles even to this day — because it is at once both revolutionary and populist.

When it was published the book was subject to fierce attack. Some stuffy academic scholars branded it as unconvincing and sentimental. Others nit-picked the story line and gleefully pointed out that the Joads came from the eastern Oklahoma town of Sallisaw, far from the scene of the actual Dust Bowl.

Zealous clergy, corporate farm landlords and politicians denounced the work as immoral and degrading. Chambers of commerce, worried about image, urged a boycott of the novel. Several school boards and libraries banned the book.

Oklahoma Congressman Lyle Boren, the son of a tenant farmer and the father of David Boren, himself a former governor and senator and the current president of the University of Oklahoma, was typical of the book's detractors. The elder Boren lambasted the novel from the floor of the House of Representatives, calling it "a lie, a black, infernal creation of a twisted, distorted mind."

Many Oklahomans read the book and liked it. Some were upset with the author and his novel, because it helped make the word, "Okie," a permanent part of the English language. The book made them feel ashamed and inferior. Actually, the term "Okie" was coined in 1907, the year Oklahoma became a state.

In truth, it should have made them feel proud. For that is what the term Okie has come to mean. Not a

badge of shame, but a badge of courage. There are
no more resilient and resourceful people on this
planet than the good stock folks from Oklahoma.
This holds true for those from generations before us
who did journey west to rebuild their lives, and for
those others who spit in the dust, who survived the
tenant farm system, and made a go of it.

It doesn't matter a hoot if Steinbeck took some
artistic liberties with geography and sociological fact.
Even back in 1939, it was obvious that any errors
Steinbeck made were totally incidental to the import
of *The Grapes of Wrath*.

This single work that speaks so eloquently to a
multitude of human experiences won the Pulitzer
Prize in 1940 and that same year became the subject
of John Ford's film classic of the same name, starring

the young Henry Fonda as Tom Joad. This novel
that has been both praised and damned, became the
cornerstone for Steinbeck's 1962 Nobel Prize Award.

And, in accepting that honor, Steinbeck uttered
words that should serve as the credo for any of us
who make our living as writers. He said:

"The ancient commission of the writer has not
changed. He is charged with exposing our many
grievous faults and failures, with dredging up to the
light our dark and dangerous dreams for the purpose
of improvement."

My friends please never forget the words of Tom
Joad, near the book's end when he says so long to his
mother, the family's rock of strength and courage.

Ma Joad asks him what he'll do, where he'll go. She says to her boy "Then what, Tom?"

And Tom says:

"Then it don't matter. Then I'll be all aroun' in the dark. I'll be ever'where — wherever you look. Whenever they's a fight so hungry people can eat, I'll be there. Whenever they's a cop beatin' up a guy, I'll be there... I'll be in the way guys yell when they're mad an' — I'll be in the way kids laugh when they're hungry an' they know supper's ready. And when our folks eat the stuff they raise an' live in the houses they build — why, I'll be there."

Like ol' Merle Haggard, be proud to be an Okie, whether or not you hail from Muskogee. If you have never read Steinbeck's book then I suggest you do.

Savor this portrait of the conflict between the powerful and the powerless, of one man's fierce reaction to injustice, and of one woman's stoical strength. This novel not only captures the horrors of the Great Depression, it probes the very nature of equality and justice in America. This book celebrates what's good about Oklahoma — this microcosm of the nation that constantly strives to find its rhythm, keep its balance, and maintain a sense of place.

Here is my summary of this land from an essay I wrote entitled "Searching for Hidden Rhythms in Twilight Land."

Oklahoma is tall grass prairie and everlasting Mountains.

Is is secret patches of ancient earth tromped smooth and hard by generations of dancing feet. It is the cycle of song and heroic deed. It is calloused hands. It is the aroma of rich crude oil fused with the scent of sweat and sacred smoke. It is the progeny of an oil-field whore wed to a deacon; the sire of a cow pony bred with a racehorse. It is a stampede, a pie supper, and a revival. It is a wildcat gusher coming in. It is a million-dollar deal cemented with a handshake.

Oklahoma is dark rivers snaking through red, furrowed soil, lakes rimmed with stone bluffs. It is the ghosts of proud Native Americans, crusading Socialists, ambitious cattle kings, extravagant oil tycoons, wily bandits. It is impetuous and it is wise. A land of opportunists, resilient pioneers, and vanquished souls, the state is a crazy quilt of contradictions and controversies, travails and triumphs. It has been exploited and abused, cherished and fought over. It is a puzzling place.

Forever Oklahoma is American through and through.

This land has plenty of scar tissue, much to brag about, and a bright future. It is an unfinished story — a work in progress.

I will close by sharing another story that speaks to the importance of having a sense of place. Again, I go back to that sense of place. It cannot be ignored or avoided.

I really learned that on an October morning filled with sunshine and promise a few years past. Suzanne and I drove to Sequoyah County in eastern Oklahoma to attend a Literary Landmark ceremony honoring Sequoyah, the Cherokee scholar who created a syllabary for his people and for whom the county was named. The ceremony was to be held ten miles northeast of Sallisaw at the one-room cabin built of hand hewn logs by Sequoyah in 1829. En route Suzanne and I talked about some of our previous trips to the historic cabin and to the many other sites in the area I visited so many times while writing my biography of Charles Arthur "Pretty Boy"

Floyd. Floyd was the consummate Oklahoma bandit, still remembered and often revered by the hardworking country folks who pass down stories about Pretty Boy like heirloom china.

Just a short ways down the turnpike a lone monarch butterfly flew into the windshield with a splat and became tangled in a windshield wiper blade. We were saddened to see the tiny creature end its short life in such a way. We knew that this was the precise time when the last generation of monarchs of summer make their incredible journey of thousands of miles southward from as far north as Canada to their wintering grounds. This was the time they fly over the landscape and when they dance across old Indian Territory just as they have forever.

The monarchs come to rest at Pismo Beach and Big

Sur in California and others go even farther and congregate by the millions deep in the mountains of Mexico, where they cloak fir trees and cluster on boughs. There they rest all winter and when they flex and flash their orange and black wings to soak up the sun the firs appear to be trimmed with jewels. In the spring when it is time to move northward again the butterflies cascade from the trees in a cloud bomb — waterfalls of sable and saffron.

Our conversation turned back to memories of coming this way with friends now gone and of other times but each of us could not help but see the monarch whose journey had ended unceremoniously on the car windshield. I knew Suzanne was especially touched since she was at the wheel, which meant she felt that she was in some way culpable for the butterfly's death.

At Sallisaw we made a pit stop at a convenience store. While I fetched waters, Suzanne got out of the car and carefully lifted the wiper blade and placed the crumpled monarch in her palm. I took over as driver and Suzanne said she wanted to make a stop before we reached the event site. I knew in a heartbeat where she wanted me to go.

Without a word being spoken, I turned off the highway and into the Akins Cemetery. This quiet country graveyard was where the largest funeral in state history took place on another October morning in 1934 when the slain Pretty Boy came home and was laid to rest with other family members. We had visited the graveyard many times and it seemed so familiar as we walked through formations of the dead marked by stones. We went directly to the Floyd plot where Pretty Boy lies next to his baby brother E. W.

Floyd, remembered as one of the best sheriffs ever in Oklahoma. As we stood there Suzanne gently placed the monarch on Pretty Boy's granite tombstone. It was as if she were leaving the outlaw who will be 30-years-old forever a flower or remembrance.

I can never explain what happened next. In only seconds, the monarch lifted its wings. The wings seemed whole and caught the sunshine. Then suddenly the butterfly rose from the stone and fluttered above us before flying off to the south. Neither of us could speak. We just stood there with our mouths open and tears welling in our eyes. We watched the monarch until it was out of sight.

Then we went on the few short miles to the cabin where Cherokee tribal leaders, dignitaries, and citizens gathered to honor Sequoyah, a wise man who himself went south to Mexico and never returned. His bones are said to remain there in the warm sand. When I rose to speak during the ceremony I told the story of the monarch. I was compelled to share it. When I finished I saw many of the Cherokee people there were nodding and some smiled. It seemed to me that they were not surprised by my simple story of resurrection.

Later when I took time to consider the day, I understood the reaction. A Cherokee elder once told me that a butterfly brings special blessings when it passes over you. In some American Indian tribes, butterflies are thought to be the departed souls of ancestors. The emergence of the adult butterfly from a cocoon symbolizes the freedom of the soul. The butterfly metamorphous is the greatest transformation in the animal world and stands as a symbol of new life, of change.

Like monarchs, the people of this land have known long and arduous journeys. Like the fragile butterflies, Oklahomans have endured much and never given up. Many have left on their own pilgrimages and traveled far. Some do not return but others come home. They keep their sense of place.

In my studio in Tulsa are my best icons and treasures — a piece of wood that was once part of Woody Guthrie's home, D. H. Lawrence's double-headed ax, buffalo skulls from Woolaroc, Pretty Boy Floyd's death mask, my grandfather's soldier medals inside a wooden necktie box, branding irons from the 101 Ranch, tarnished deputy sheriff badges, a lucky coyote fang from No Man's Land, a Phillips 66 sign riddled with Okie bullet holes, a Mother Road shield. There's a jug of genuine Creek County stump liquor, a hangman's noose from Fort Smith, battered typewriters, baseballs bearing the signatures of boyhood heroes, stacks of books, mounds of letters, diaries, photos, and memories. Memories galore.

From my windows I see the Arkansas flowing past and I dare to dream. I spy the old bridge that links east and west. Sometimes, from the corner of my eye, I catch a glimpse of an angel in disguise. And I look beyond the great oaks and magnolias, beyond the river and the bridge, to the eternal and everlasting West. It is then that I know the truth of this place — I feel it in my heart and in my bones.

I am home.

TULSA TOWN HALL

Tulsa Town Hall is a non-profit, educational, cultural organization that has been bringing nationally and internationally prominent speakers to Tulsa since 1935. Town Hall was started by a small group of Tulsa women and over the years has grown and evolved from a beginning capacity of 400 at the Ritz Theater (with luncheon following in the Crystal Ballroom at the Mayo Hotel) to a capacity of over 2300 in the Chapman Music Hall of the Performing Arts Center in downtown Tulsa.

Since the founding of Tulsa Town Hall many prestigious speakers have been featured including

Thorton Wilder, Sinclair Lewis, Edna St. Vincent Millay, Will Durant, Thomas Mann, Thomas Hart Benton, Norman Cousins, Helen Hayes, Ralph Nader, Charles Kuralt, and Maya Angelou.

For more on Tulsa Town Hall, visit http://www.tulsatownhall.com.

MICHAEL WALLIS

It has been said, "reading a Michael Wallis book is like dancing to a romantic ballad. He offers his hand and gently guides you across the floor, swaying to the song of the American West."

A best-selling author and award-winning reporter, Michael is a historian and biographer of the American West who also has gained international notoriety as a speaker and voice talent. In 2006 Michael's distinctive voice was heard in *Cars*, an animated feature film from Pixar Studios, also featuring Paul Newman, Bonnie Hunt, Owen Wilson, Michael Keaton, and George Carlin.

Michael is also featured in *Cars 2*, a sequel to the original motion picture released in 2011.

A storyteller who likes nothing better than transporting audiences across time and space, Michael has published seventeen books, including *Route 66: The Mother Road*, the book credited with sparking the resurgence of interest in the highway. In 2011, Michael's latest works were published — *David Crockett: The Lion of the West*, and *The Wild West 365*.

Other Wallis books include *The Real Wild West: The 101 Ranch and the Creation of the American West; Mankiller: A Chief and Her People; Way Down Yonder In The Indian Nation;* and *Pretty Boy: The Life and Times of Charles Arthur Floyd*. His work has been published in hundreds of national and international magazines and newspapers, including Time, Life, People, Smithsonian, The New Yorker, and The New York Times.

Michael has been nominated three times for the Pulitzer Prize and was also a nominee for the National Book Award. He has won many other prestigious honors, such as the Will Rogers Spirit Award, the Western Heritage Award from the National Cowboy Hall & Western Heritage Museum, the Oklahoma Book Award from the Oklahoma Center for the Book, and the Best Western Non-fiction Award from the Western Writers of America.

To connect with Michael Wallis online, visit http://www.michaelwallis.com.

ALSO BY MICHAEL WALLIS

Oil Man: The Story of Frank Phillips and the Birth of Phillips Petroleum ✦ *Route 66: The Mother Road* ✦ *Pretty Boy: The Life and Times of Charles Arthur Floyd* ✦ *Way Down Yonder in the Indian Nation: Writings from America's Heartland* ✦ *Mankiller: A Chief and Her People* (with Wilma Mankiller) ✦ *En Divina Luz: The Penitente Moradas of New Mexico* ✦ *Beyond The Hills: The Journey of Waite Phillips* ✦ *Songdog Diary: 66 Stories From the Road* (with Suzanne Fitzgerald Wallis) ✦ *Oklahoma Crossroads* ✦ *The Real Wild West: The 101 Ranch and the Creation of the American West* ✦ *Heaven's Window: A Journey Through Northern New Mexico* ✦ *Hogs on Route 66* (with Marian Clark) ✦

The Art of Cars (with Suzanne Fitzgerald Wallis) ◆
Billy the Kid: The Endless Rise ◆ *The Lincoln
Highway: Coast to Coast from Times Square to the
Golden Gate* ◆ *David Crockett: The Lion of the West* ◆
The Wild West: 365 Days (with Suzanne Fitzgerald
Wallis)

GET THE EBOOK, FREE!

At Digitature, we want you to enjoy this book in whatever format you like, whenever you like. Leave your print book at home and take the eBook to go! Purchase the print edition and receive the eBook free. Just send an email to ebook@digitature.com and include:

- The book title.
- The name of the store where you purchased it.
- Your receipt number.
- Your preference of file type: PDF or ePub?

A real person will respond to your email with your eBook attached. Thank you for supporting an independently owned publisher with your purchase!

Made in the USA
Lexington, KY
16 May 2012